King Midas and His Golden Touch

Children's Greek & Roman Myths

BABY PROFESSOR

EDUCATION KIDS

The story of King
Midas is about what
happens when people
do not know what
true happiness is.

Midas wished
that everything
he touched would
turn into gold. But,
he did not think
through what he
was asking for. He
did not understand
that getting this wish
would be a curse,
not a blessing.

Here is how the
story goes:

Midas was a rich
king who already
had a great fortune.
He ruled the
country of Phrygia,
in Asia Minor. He
had everything a
king could wish for.

He lived in a large, luxurious palace. He had a beautiful daughter with whom he shared his life of abundance.

Even though he was very rich, he was not content. Midas thought that his greatest happiness was provided by gold. His favorite hobby was counting and re-counting his golden coins! He occasionally used to cover his body with gold objects, as if he was swimming in them. Money was his obsession.

One day, the god of wine and revelry, Dionysus, passed through the kingdom of Midas. A satyr named Silenus, one of Dionysus' companions, got delayed along the way.

Silenus was tired and decided to take a nap in the famous rose gardens surrounding the palace of King Midas. The king found him there and Midas, recognizing him, invited Silenus to spend a few days at his palace.

Then Midas took Silenus to Dionysus. The god of celebration was very grateful for Midas' kindness and promised Midas that he grant any wish Midas had. Midas thought for a while and then finally said, "I want that everything I touch becomes gold."

Dionysus warned the king that his wish was unwise, but Midas was insistent. So, Dionysus promised the king that, starting the following day, everything he touched would turn into gold.

The next day, Midas woke up early and was very eager to see if his wish had come true. He extended his arm and touched a table that immediately turned into gold. He was very happy and jumped up and down!

He then touched
the carpet, a
chair, the door,
a table, his
bathtub, and they
turned to gold!
He ran all over
his palace until
he got exhausted
and happy at
the same time!

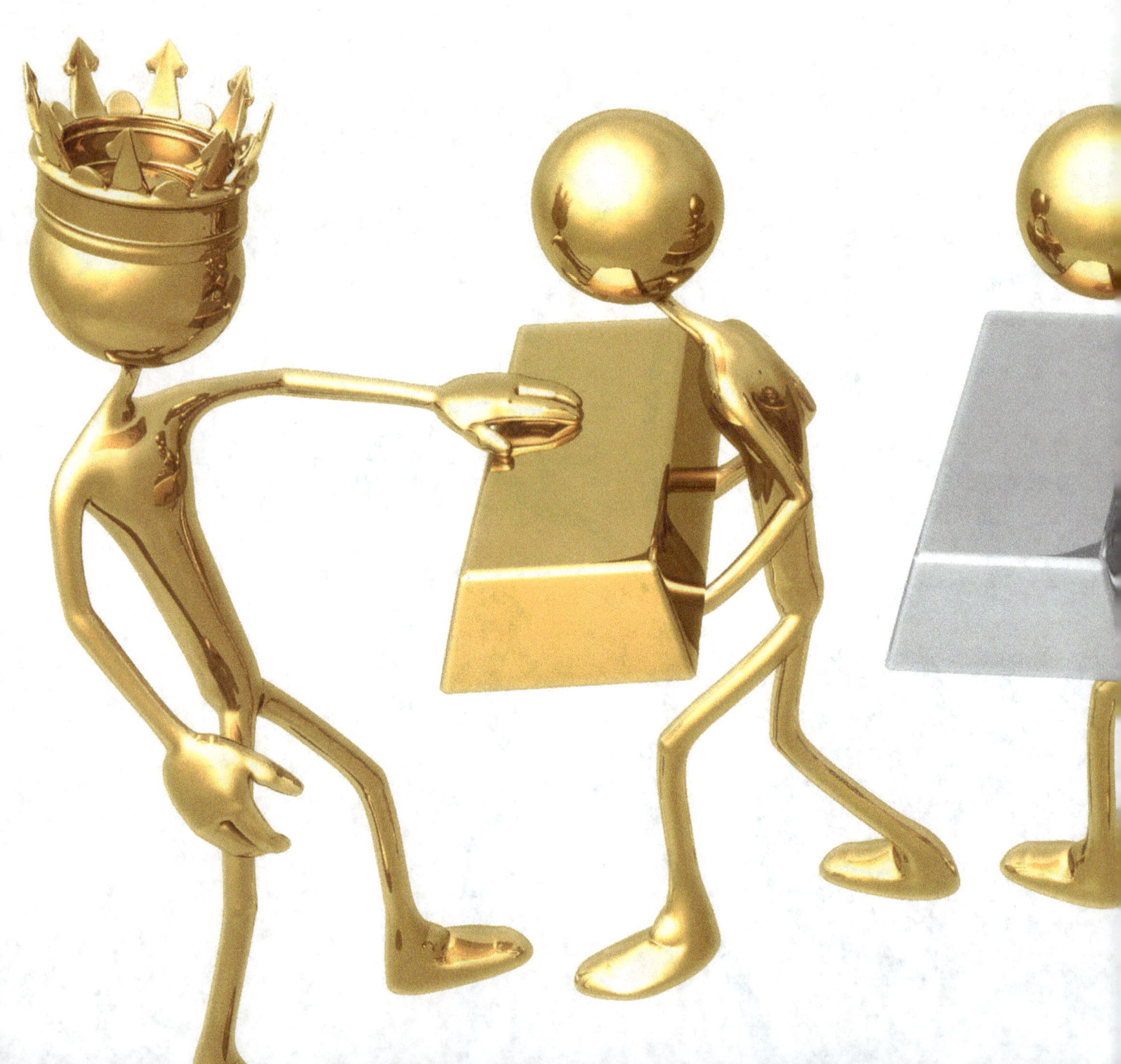

He then sat at the table to have his breakfast. He took a rose between his hands to smell its fragrance. However when he touched the rose, it became gold. He thought in disappointment, "I suppose I will have to smell the fragrance without touching the roses."

Without even thinking, he ate a grape but it also turned into gold! The same happened with the bread and the glass of water.

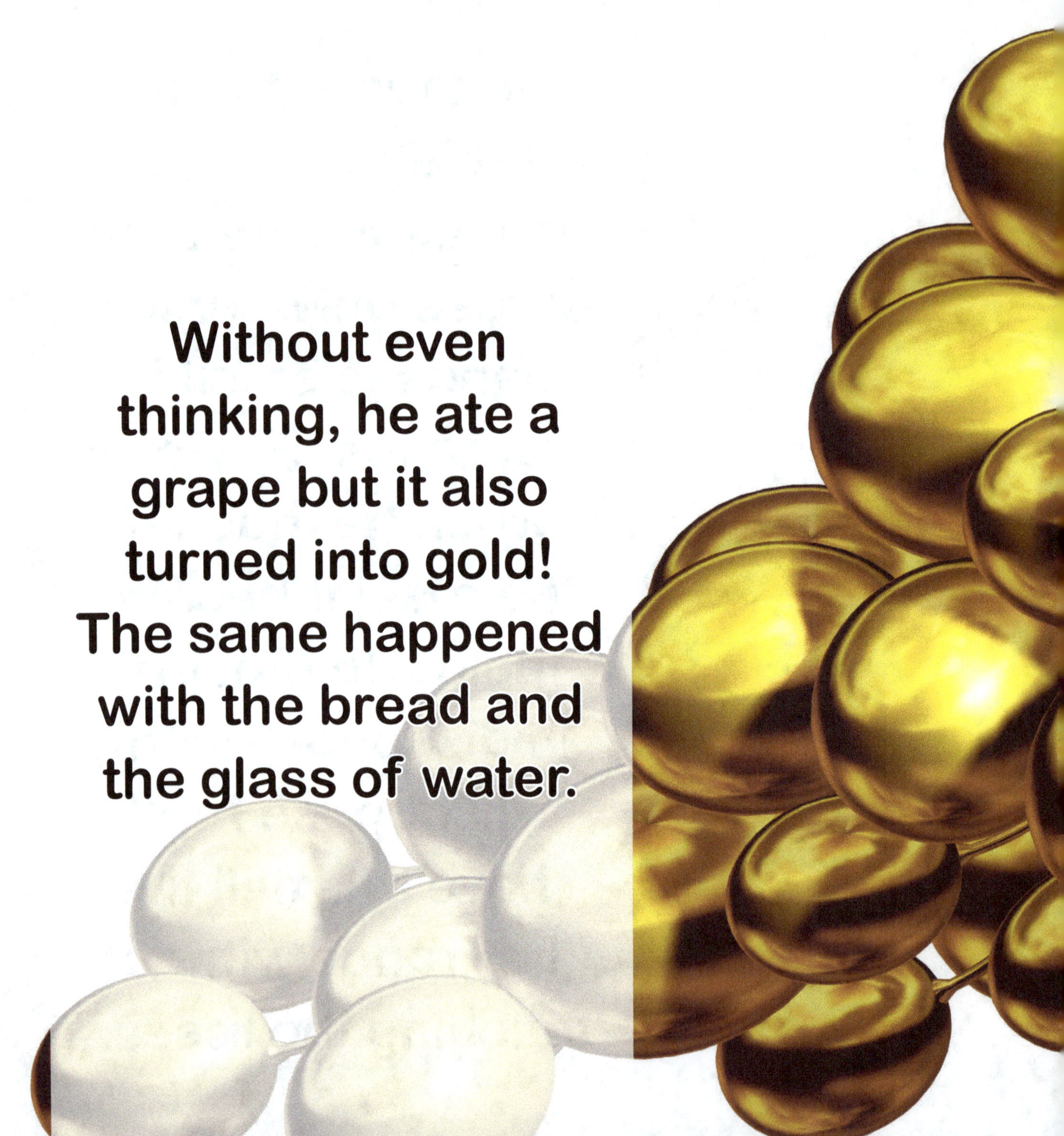

He started to sense fear. Tears filled his eyes. His beloved daughter entered the room at that moment. When Midas hugged her, she turned into a golden statue. He fell into despair because of what he had done. Then he raised his arms and prayed to the god Dionysus to take the curse from him.

The god heard
Midas and told
him to go to the
river Pactolus and
wash his hands
there. Midas
did so: he ran
to the river and
was amazed to
see gold flowing
from his hands.

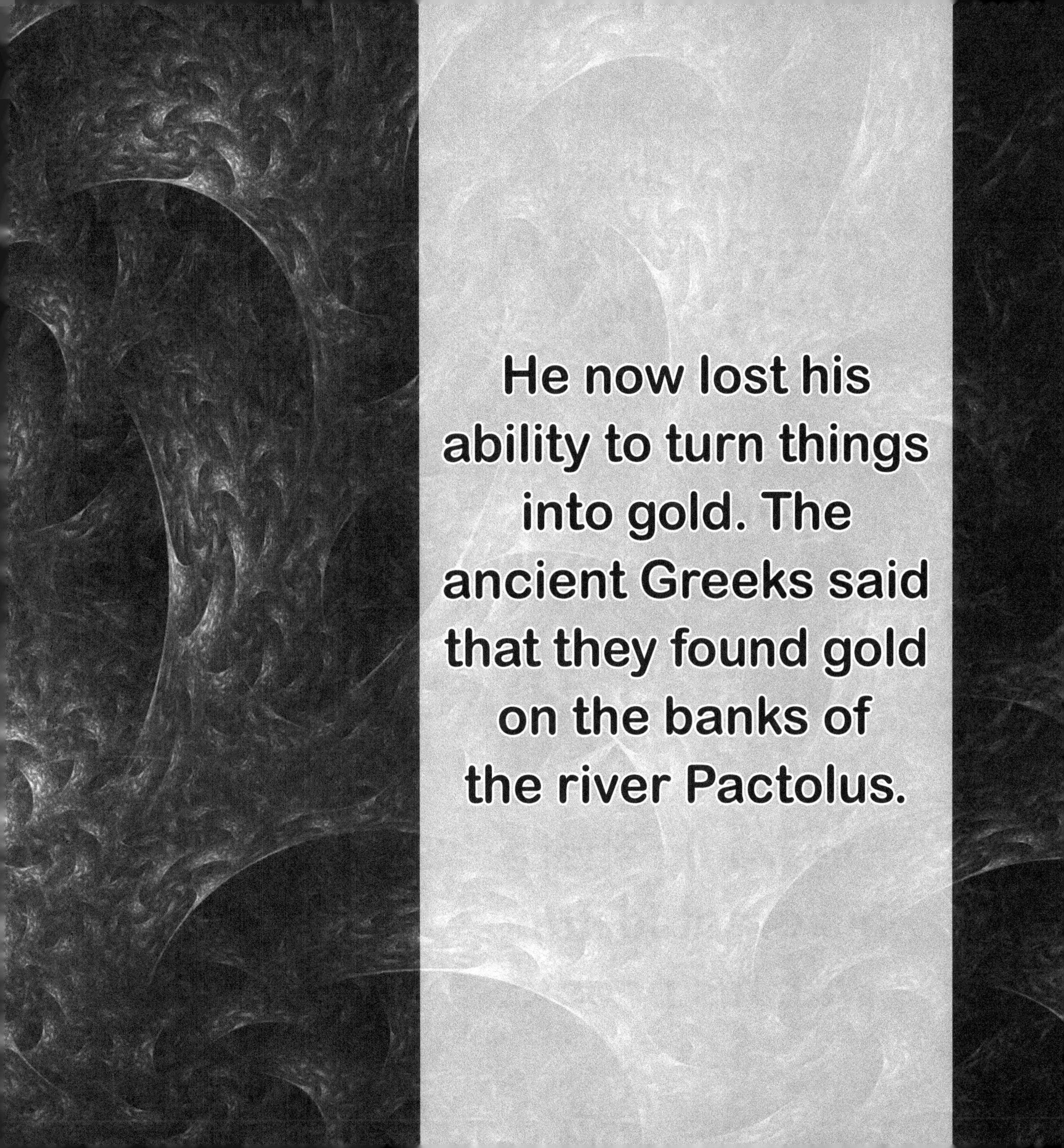

He now lost his
ability to turn things
into gold. The
ancient Greeks said
that they found gold
on the banks of
the river Pactolus.

When Midas
returned home,
everything he
had touched
had become
normal again.
Midas hugged
his daughter in
full happiness
and decided that
he would share
his great fortune
with his people.

From that time, Midas became a better person. He became generous and grateful for all the good things in his life. His people led a prosperous life, and when he died they all mourned for their beloved king.

We can learn from
this myth that greed
could bring negative
results that may
lead us to become
slaves on our own
selfish desires.
From this myth,
we got the phrase
'Midas touch', which
usually means that
the person can
make unlikely things
become valuable.

Visit
BABY PROFESSOR
EDUCATION KIDS
www.BabyProfessorBooks.com
to download Free Baby Professor eBooks
and view our catalog of new and exciting
Children's Books